new fashion designers'
sketchbooks

RUTH ASAWA

~Woven Sculptures~

EGGS

in detail

TRACEY COLLINS

—The Tree Restaurant (New Zeland)

BUTTERFLY

ZARIDA ZAMAN

new fashion designers'
sketchbooks

A&CB

First published in 2011 by
A&C Black Publishers, an imprint of
Bloomsbury Publishing Plc
50 Bedford Square
London WC1B 3DP
www.bloomsbury.com

CIP Catalogue records for this book are available
from the British Library and the US Library of
Congress.

Book design by Bradbury and Williams
Cover design by Sutchinda Thompson
Publisher: Susan James

ISBN 978-14081-4062-8

This book is produced using paper that is made
from wood grown in managed, sustainable
forests. It is natural, renewable and recyclable.
The logging and manufacturing processes
conform to the environmental regulations of the
country of origin.

Printed and bound in China.

Picture credits:
Pages 1,2-3,7: Elena Occidente
Page 4: Crimson O'Shea

contents

foreword

ZARIDA ZAMAN'S BOOK ON THE ROLE that the sketchbook plays in the fashion design process will be of real value to any aspiring fashion design student. It gives tangible insight into the crucial role that drawing inspiration from a variety of sources and the subsequent exploration of these ideas in a personal notebook plays in the creative thinking and fashion design process. A sketchbook enables the designer to build a series of reference materials that will play a crucial role throughout their career. A sketchbook allows the designer to play with materials and colours as they have an ongoing dialogue with themselves about the ideas and references that inspire them. It is this experimentation, in a personal and often very private notebook, that allows the designer to test and develop their concepts, and build a particular perspective that will ultimately form the basis for a new collection, approach to design, textiles or styling. What is so pertinent and helpful about Zarida's publication is that it draws on the sketchbooks of a number of fashion designers. It thereby shows how varied and personal sketchbooks can and should be. I hope it will inspire anyone interested in developing a career in fashion to experiment with a wide range of source materials, colours, mark making techniques and ideas.

PROFESSOR FRANCES CORNER OBE
HEAD OF COLLEGE, LONDON COLLEGE OF FASHION

introduction

THE IDEA FOR THE BOOK came about one day when I realised while teaching my students, I had nothing to show them about how to work in research sketchbooks, other than work held back from previous years' students. That was when I realised the need for something that documented the process and could be shared with young fashion designers around the world.

The process of working and researching in a sketchbook is universal and unchanging, whether you are designing a chair, a car or a skirt. When I teach, I often discuss with my students what they believe the importance of research is. Eventually they realise that without research, there would be no new ideas.

I often find research can be the most exciting part of any project. It's the space where you learn and discover and grow. The freedom of gathering research in a research sketchbook allows you to explore the unexpected and to develop your ideas with no limitations, restrictions or predictions.

As a student, I found the process of working in a research sketchbook a big change from the way I was used to working. Instead of writing and composing essays to demonstrate my knowledge, I had to learn something totally new. I had to learn to visually communicate my thoughts and ideas. Suddenly, everything was exposed and there was nowhere to hide my ideas. After much trial and error I eventually got used to working this way, it all made perfect sense and there was no going back.

It was around that time that I become a hoarder. I kept everything from brightly coloured sweet wrappers, random swatches of fabric and an eclectic collection of postcards. I didn't really know why I was keeping these random things, I just knew that one day I would need them for a page in a research sketchbook. And one day I usually did. Many research sketchbooks later, working this way eventually allowed me to find my own voice when it came to developing ideas and designing clothes. A guilty secret of fashion designers lies in the knowledge of the wealth of ideas that exist within research sketchbooks that will never see the light of day. Ideas thought to be un-wearable, un-makeable and quite simply, outlandish are both the brilliance and tragedy of research sketchbooks.

Over the years I have found the creative process of research never-ending. There is always more to learn, more to see, more to find out about and more to have an opinion about. It's a never ending process.

In this book I have tried to document the process of how research develops, from initial ideas through to the ideas for clothing or accessories. The process happens in different ways for different people. There is no right or wrong. Just a question of 'which way do you go now?'

ZARIDA ZAMAN

laura faye athey

LAURA USES THE RESEARCH PROCESS TO RECORD AND INTERPRET WHAT SHE SEES THROUGH DRAWING. HER RESEARCH SKETCHBOOK IS A VISUAL DIARY TO REFLECT BACK AND RE-EVALUATE HER THOUGHTS. THE PROCESS EVOLVES IN A THOUGHTFUL AND NATURAL WAY. CONTEXTUAL REFERENCES FOUND IN THE WORK OF OTHER ARTISTS HELP HER EXPAND HER IDEAS AND PROVIDE INSPIRATION FOR HER WORK ON THE FEMALE MANNEQUIN STAND.

stel la
mc cartney
spring
2011

Fruit and Vegetable
Sculptures

<< *My research is very important because*
it is my diary of creative thoughts put down through drawings.
Without it, my designs would have little meaning to me >>

madeleine ayres

MADELEINE TAKES HER RESEARCH SKETCHBOOK WITH HER WHEREVER SHE GOES, DRAWING AND WRITING ABOUT ANYTHING THAT INSPIRES HER. SHE USES DRAWING AND WRITING AS ESSENTIAL PARTS OF THE RESEARCH PROCESS. SHE WORKS BY DEVELOPING HER IDEAS THROUGH 3D EXPERIMENTS, VISUAL IMAGERY AND STORYTELLING. SHE LIKES TO EXHAUST ALL POSSIBILITIES BEFORE CONCLUDING HER WORK.

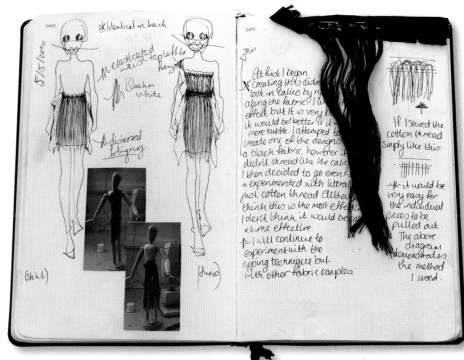

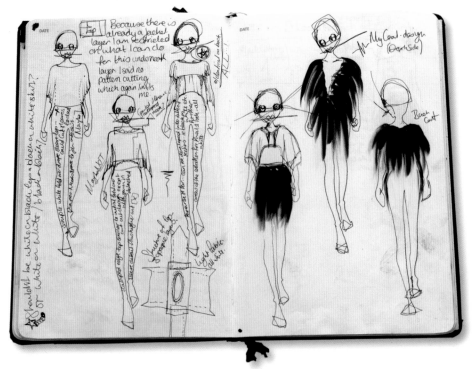

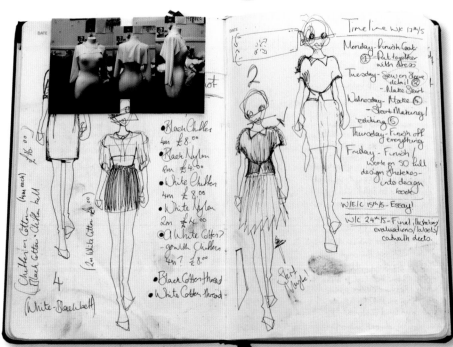

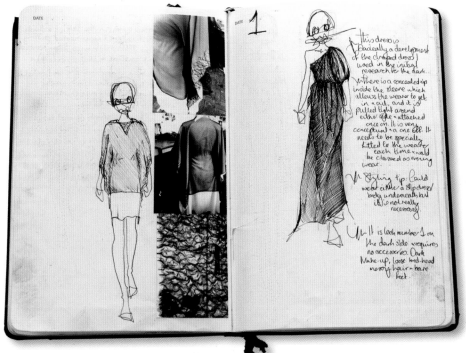

This dress is basically a development of the draped dress I used in the initial research for the dark.

There is a concealed zip inside the sleeve which allows the wearer to get in + out, and it is pulled tight around either side + attached once on. It is very conceptual + a one off. It needs to be specially fitted to the wearer each time + would be classed as evening wear.

Styling tip: Could wear either a slip dress/body underneath but it is not really necessary.

It is look number 1 on the dark side + requires no accessories. Dark Make-up, loose bed-head messy hair + bare feet.

<< *The more I research, the more I discover and the more informed and individual my designs become. The research process is a journey and I love learning new things* >>

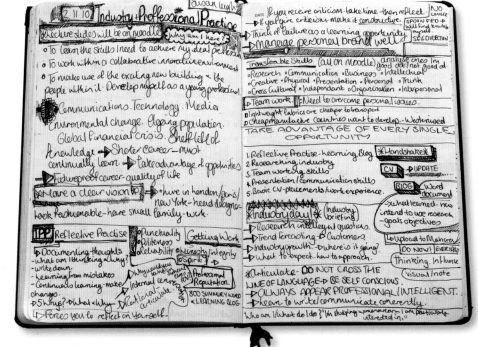

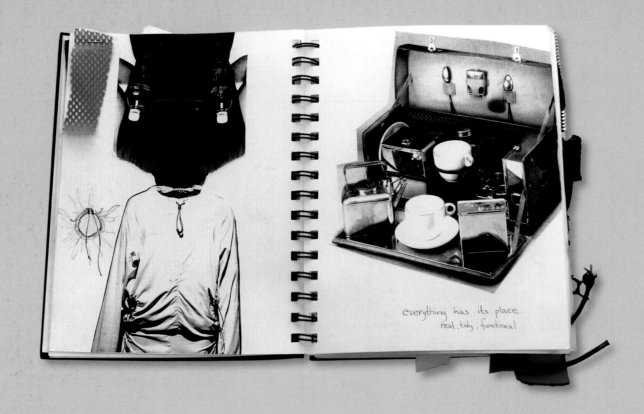

everything has its place.
neat, tidy, functional

Hampus Berggen
HAMPUS TAKES INSPIRATION FROM THE PRACTICAL SIDE OF GARMENTS AND ACCESSORIES AND MARRIES THE TWO TOGETHER TO PRODUCE CLOTHING WHICH IS WEARABLE AND FUNCTIONAL. HIS RESEARCH DELVES INTO THE TRADITIONAL ASPECTS AND HE REINTERPRETS WITH DESIGNS THAT HAVE A MODERN TWIST.

parachute.

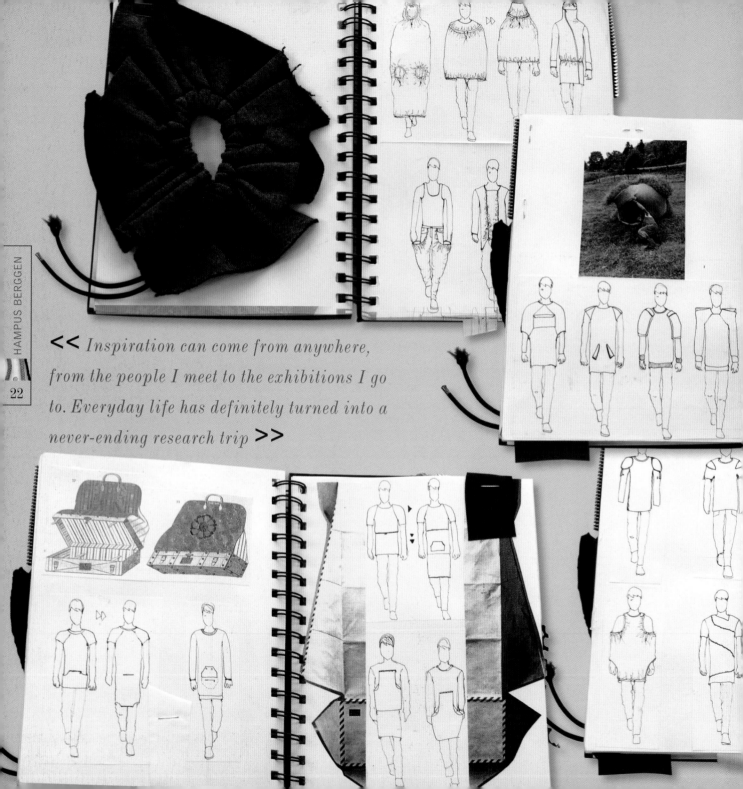

<< *Inspiration can come from anywhere, from the people I meet to the exhibitions I go to. Everyday life has definitely turned into a never-ending research trip* >>

PHOENIX HALL

BODHISATTVA RAISED BY CLOUDS

SOFT, FLUFFY CLOUDS,
BUT REPRESENTED IN
STONE & STRUCTURED.

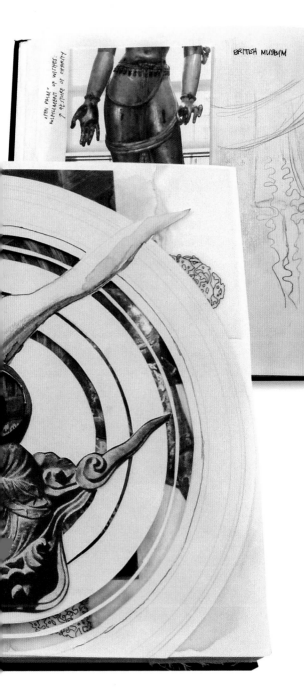

BRITISH MUSEUM

BUDDHIST
HAND SYMBOLS

jessica ng comer DETAILS OF

CLOTHING ARE USED AS INSPIRATION FOR IDEAS.
WRAPPING IDEAS ARE MIXED WITH MODERN
SCULPTURE INFLUENCES, AND THE COMBINATION OF
RESULTS IS AN UNUSUAL CLASHING OF CULTURES.
JESSICA ENJOYS RESEARCH THAT CHALLENGES
THE NORM BY PLACING TWO OPPOSING SUBJECTS
TOGETHER AND SEEING THE JOURNEY OF HER
RESEARCH DEVELOP INTO SOMETHING UNEXPECTED.

SHAOLIN MONKS.

FD FABRIC IN MOTION.

teal glaze   eggplant rsc

sunshine yellow   electric blue

CONICAL SHAPE

DIFF. PANELS
OF LAYERED FABRIC
APPEARS DRAPED.

BRITISH MUSEUM
- STONEWARE FROM JUDGEMENT GROUP
- MING DYNASTY 16TH c. AD
- ONE OF THE JUDGES OF HELL
  HOLDING SCROLL OF GOOD DEEDS.

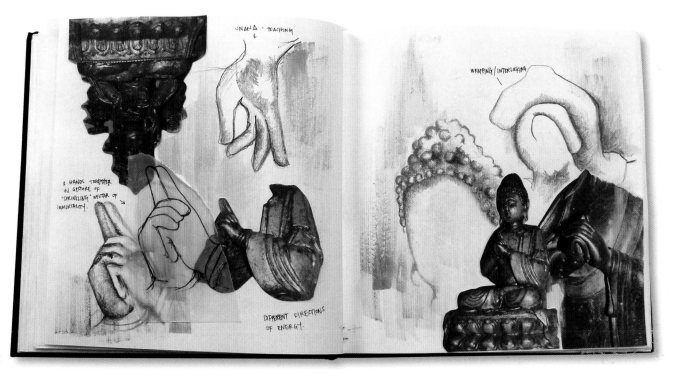

ANANDA : TEACHING

WRAPPING / INTERLOCKING

2 HANDS TOGETHER IN GESTURE OF "SPRINKLING" NECTAR OF IMMORTALITY.

DIFFERENT DIRECTIONS OF ENERGY.

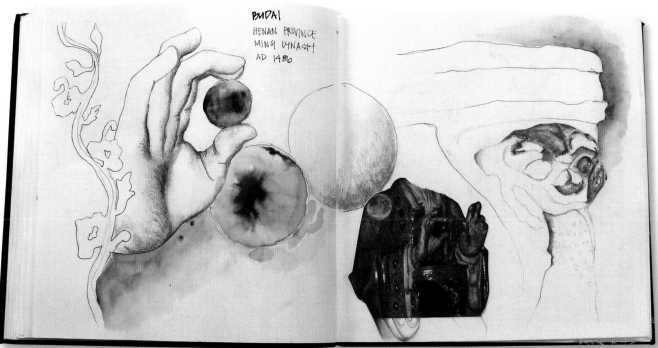

BUDAI
HENAN PROVINCE
MING DYNASTY
AD 1486

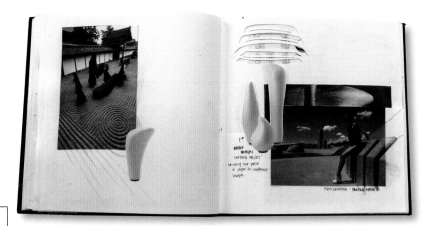

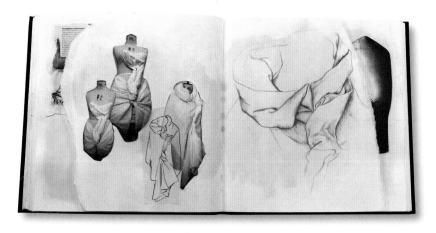

AUDREY KAWASAKI

<< *I find inspiration in destructive and unconventional beauty. This helps me to create something that isn't obvious* >>

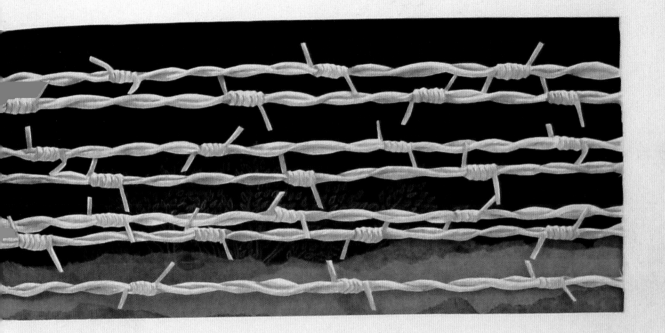

shabnam eslambolchi DIFFICULT TOPICS ARE OFTEN USED AS
THEMES FOR CREATING CLOTHING. SHABNAM DELVES INTO HER RESEARCH, WHICH
RELIES ON HISTORICAL REFERENCING AND EVENTS, TO PROVIDE VISUAL IMAGERY
AS HER INSPIRATION.
HER AIM IS TO DEVELOP IDEAS THAT STILL EVOKE THE THEME AND TO DESIGN
WEARABLE CLOTHING.

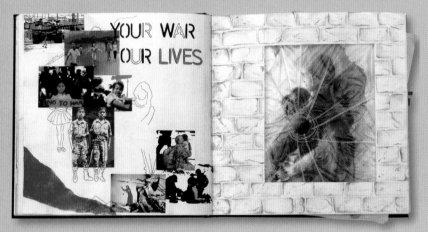

<< Sometimes themes for projects can be challenging, but the goal is to extract enough information to work towards creating an interesting collection >>

GORDON BARNES & SHELBY DAVIS

RAFFAEL RHEINSBERG

MIROSLAW BALKA

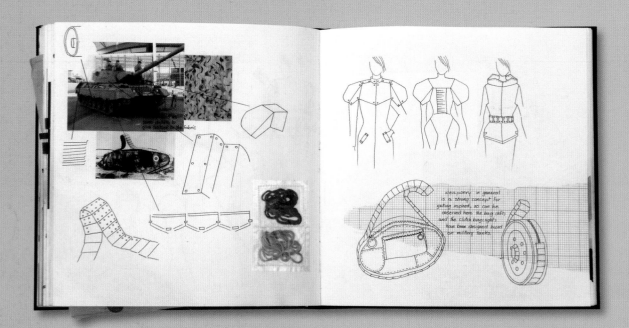

weaponry in general
is a strong concept for
getive inspired, as can be
observed here. the bag (left)
and the clutch bag (right)
have been designed based
on military tanks.

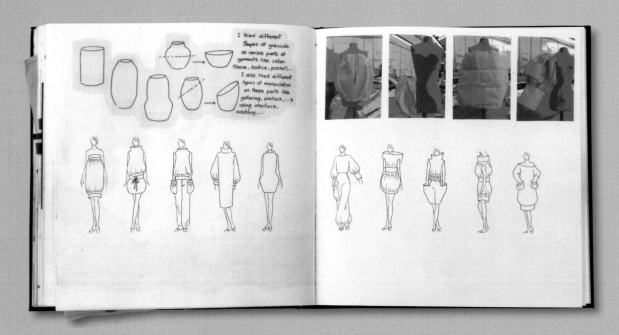

I tried different
Shapes of grenade
as various parts of
garments like collar,
Sleeve, bodice, pocket,...
I also tried different
types of manipulation
on these parts like
gathering, pintuck,... &
using interface,
wadding,....

Cubic segments in grenades can be very inspiring to add more details to a design.

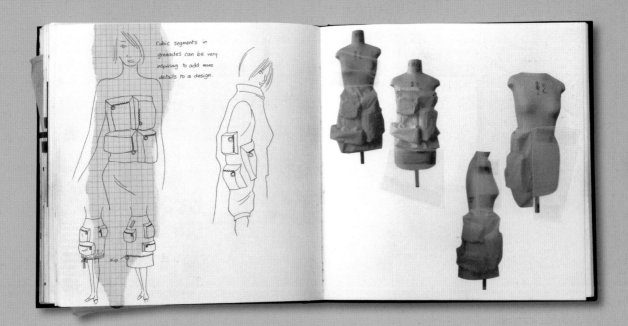

nolwenn faligot
NOLWENN USES HER INITIAL RESEARCH TO SPARK IDEAS FOR TEXTURE, FORM AND VOLUME. SHE USES EMOTIONAL RESPONSES TO HELP HER IN THE RESEARCH AND DESIGN PROCESS. HER RESEARCH IS A CONSTANT CIRCULAR JOURNEY OF GATHERING, INTERPRETING AND EXPERIMENTING WITH IDEAS.

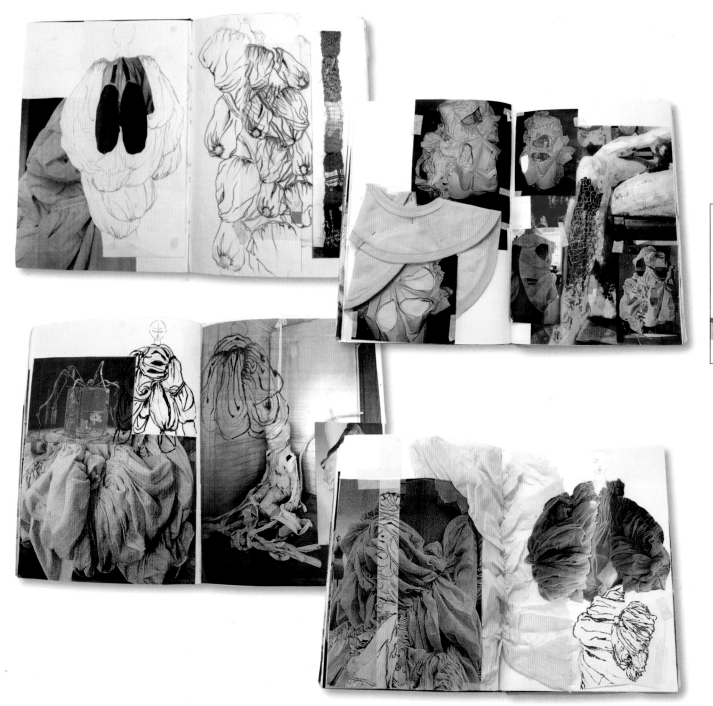

<< *I think researching is about trying to look at things in an original and personal way, this is why I am inspired mostly by my environment and experiences* >>

yuji fu YUJI FINDS INSPIRATION IN ARCHITECTURAL DETAILS, LAYERS AND CURVES. HE USES PHOTOGRAPHY TO MANIPULATE AND INTERPRET HIS THOUGHTS AND IDEAS. HE ALSO USES 3D SHAPES TO EXPERIMENT AND EXPLORE HIS IDEAS AGAINST THE MANNEQUIN STAND.

Iris Van Herpen

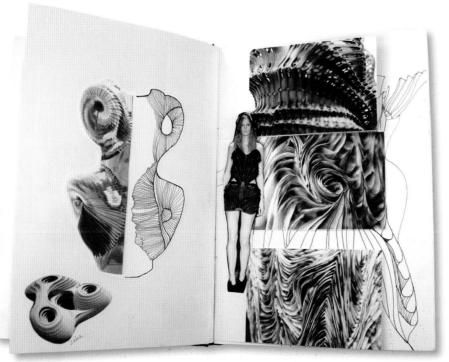

<< *I want my ideas to break the mould. Research is where that journey begins, and it's up to me where I take it* >>

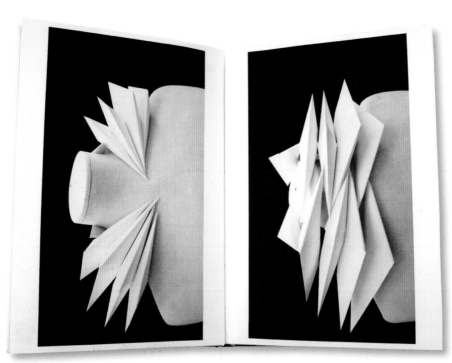

Reikawakubo/Comme des Garcons

Jun Takahashi
2006 S/S.
Dark blue brown 8.00

Yohji Yamamoto
A/W.

Reikawakubo

Yohji Yamamoto

Reikawakubo/Comme des Garcons

A/W
Junya Watanabe

jia xin gao

JIA IS A DESIGNER WHO HAS HER OWN DISTINCTIVE STYLE AND APPROACH TO DESIGNING CLOTHING. SHE USES THE RESEARCH PROCESS TO RECORD WHAT SHE SEES AND TO FIND INSPIRATION IN EVERYTHING AND ANYTHING THAT SURROUNDS HER. HER VISION AND STYLE CONTINUES TO DEVELOP AND EVOLVE AS SHE MOVES THROUGH THE CREATIVE PROCESS AND BEGINS TO FILTER HER IDEAS.

Benjamin hubert
spinning lights

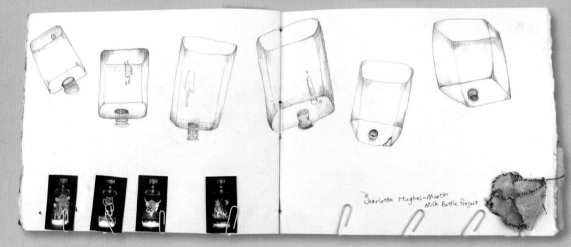

Charlotte Hughes-Martin
Milk Bottle Project

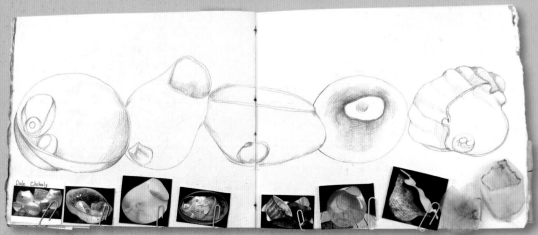

Dale Chihuly

<< *The fundamental process of research is to challenge what exists to find a new perspective and my own vision* >>

Lynch's films are known for night marsh and dreamlike images and meticulous sound design

Inland Empire is a 2006 **psychological thriller** film with elements of horror written and directed by **David Lynch**

David Lynch: "It's about a **woman in trouble**, and **it's mystery**, and that's all I want to say about it".

As a **clue** to the film Lynch gives a quotation from a translation of the **Atharva Upanishad**: "We are like the spider. We weave our life and then move along in it. We are like the dreamer who dreams and then lives in the dream. This is true for the entire universe".

Emotion is a **cause of action**

iryna gorelikova

THE FEMALE BODY IS ONE OF THE MAIN SOURCES OF INSPIRATION FOR IRYNA. WITHIN THE PROCESS OF RESEARCH SHE LOOKS FOR A STORY TO PROVIDE A NARRATIVE FOR THE JOURNEY, OFTEN FOUND THROUGH HER NATURAL ILLUSTRATIVE STYLE AND MUSES SHE CREATES ALONG THE WAY.

HER WORK IS BASED ON FINDING INTEREST IN THE UNUSUAL OR MUNDANE, SEARCHING THROUGH HISTORY TO DISCOVER SOMETHING NEW.

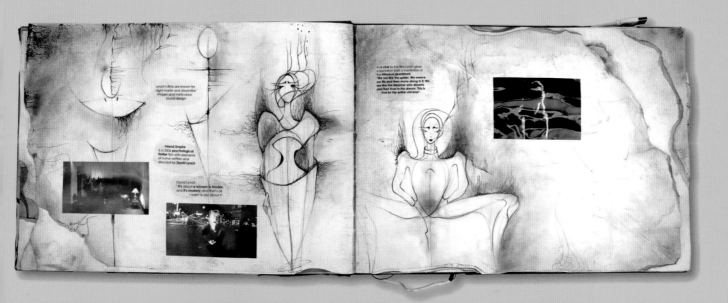

<< *The most interesting thing I find about working is that*

I never know what the outcome will be until I'm finished >>

wolfgang jarnach

FOR WOLFGANG, THE PROCESS OF RESEARCH ISN'T JUST ABOUT GOING TO MUSEUMS AND GALLERIES, IT'S ABOUT RECORDING WHAT HE SEES AS HE GETS ON WITH HIS DAY. HE ENJOYS QUESTIONING THE CONVENTIONAL AND USING THIS AS A BASIS FOR HIS MENSWEAR DESIGNS.

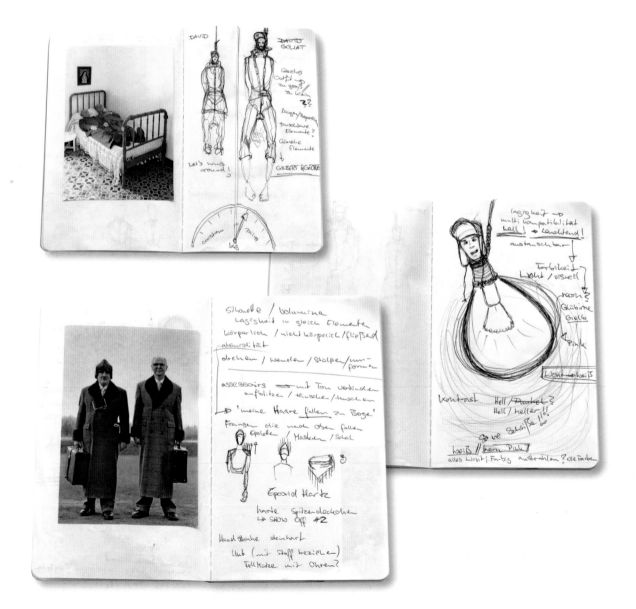

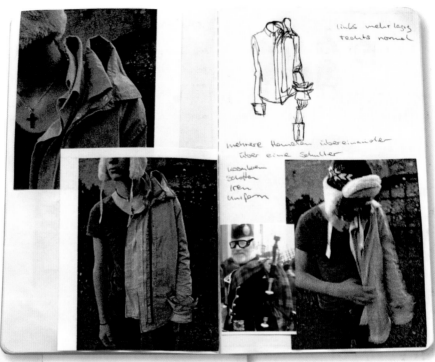

links mehr layig
rechts normal

mehrere Hemden übereinander
über eine Schulter

woanders
Schotten
Iren
uniform

- DB TRENCH mit Gürtel
  durch einen Ärmel
- Mehrlagen Hemd
  überlang /Oversize
- Shorts mit tiefem
  Schritt
- Stulpen / Leggins

IMG_0438.JPG

IMG_0440.JPG

mit Gürtel
halter
organic
strapping

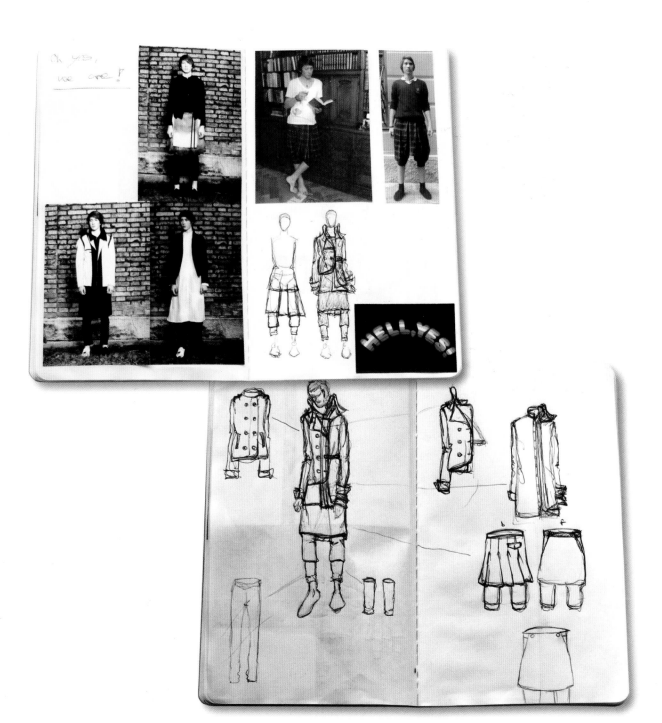

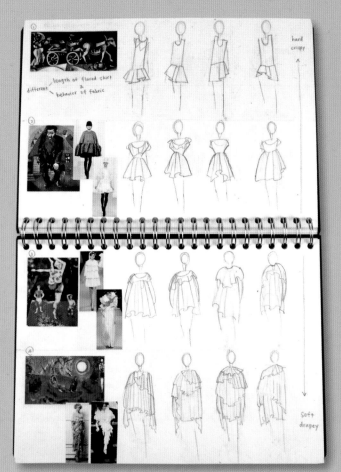

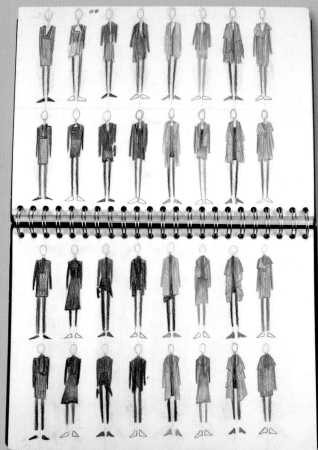

sayaka kamakura

RE-QUESTIONING AND RE-THINKING IS THE BASIS OF HOW SAYAKA APPROACHES RESEARCH. HER WORK RELIES ON EXPERIMENTATION AND DEVELOPMENT ON THE MANNEQUIN STAND. HER IDEAS ARE SIMPLE AND SHE WORKS WITH A LOGICAL, ALMOST MATHEMATICAL APPROACH TO PROBLEM-SOLVING. SHE RELIES ON HER RESEARCH TO DOCUMENT THE WHOLE OF THE PROCESS.

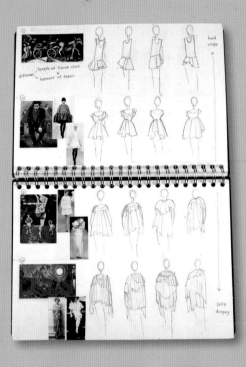

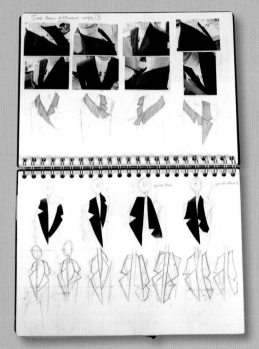

<< *Fashion design could be investigated from many viewpoints,*

such as social communication, the human body, art, and design.

My curiosity will be never-ending >>

ani tan lam

<< *I am inspired by the world around me,*

I love taking photographs from little things in life

which sometimes become part of my research >>

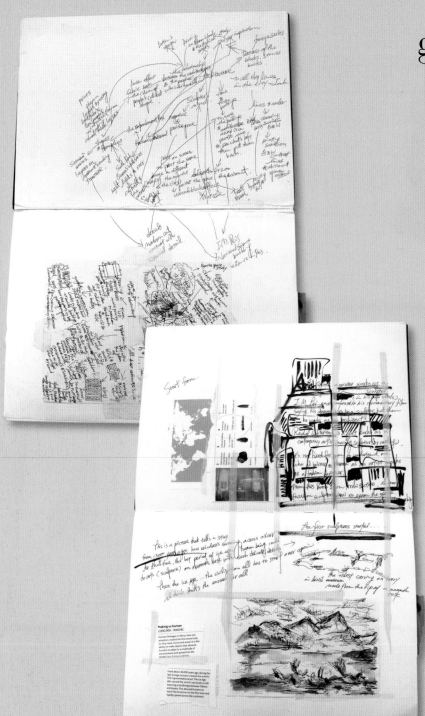

gloria lin GLORIA

BEGINS EVERY PROJECT BY COLLECTING IMAGERY RELEVANT TO HER PROJECT AND EDITING THE BEST OF WHAT SHE HAS. SHE GUIDES THE VIEWER ON A VERY PERSONAL JOURNEY THROUGH HER OWN INVESTIGATIONS AND CONCLUSIONS, CREATING COLLAGES OF IMAGERY. SHE USES HER RESEARCH TO INSPIRE IDEAS FOR FASHION SHAPES, PRINTS AND KNITWEAR.

A poetic eye

Black & White floor are
watercolor on Wood paper
Neolid texture around

to spaces

Sculptures & Architectures

Architectures speak for the city with the skyline that composed by buildings
yet, it would be a dull dialog without the juice of sculptures in between
from the roof of British Museum to the monuments in Trafalgar Square
sculptures complete the space that is loved by
fill up the composition with a touch of jewels.

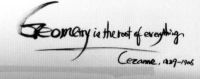

Time

From 1874, this Midland Hotel, above St Pancras Station had been one of...

St Pancras Hotel

Geometry is the root of everything

Cezanne, 1839–1906

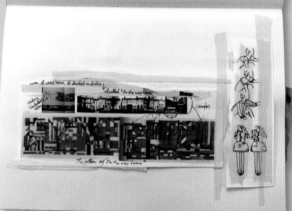

<< It's the appreciation of the small details in life that I see and I let my ideas grow organically >>

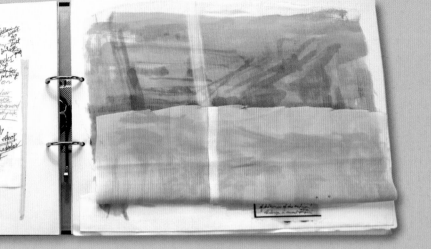

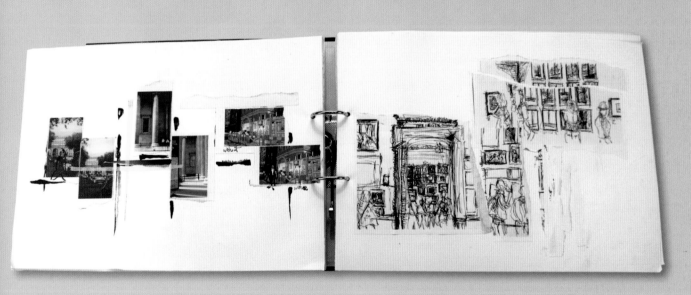

WHAT HE LIKES: SPORTS

arianna luparia ARIANNA USES HER NATURAL CREATIVE TALENTS TO
TRANSLATE WHAT SHE SEES IN AN INTERESTING AND VISUALLY CAPTIVATING WAY. SHE
DEVELOPS HER RESEARCH BY CONTEXTUALIZING HER IDEAS WITHIN THE WIDER WORLD.
SHE IMPOSES HER OWN INTERPRETATION BY CREATING A VISUAL NARRATIVE.

ARIANNA LUPARIA

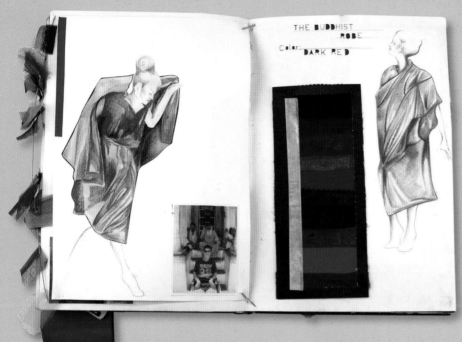

THE BUDDHIST
ROBE
Color: DARK RED

<< *I always carry my camera around, so every day is a research day for me* >>

The Robes of Buddhist Monks.
The robe comes from the idea of wearing cheap clothes just to protect the body from weather and climate.
Since DARK RED was the cheapest colour in Kashmir they have red robes.

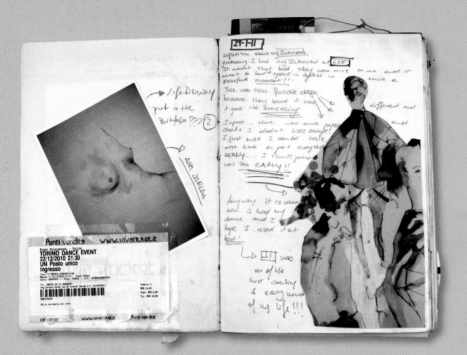

Life Drawing → put in the Portfolio ??? ②

→ ASK ZARALA

Punti vendita   www.vivaticket.it
TORINO DANCE EVENT
22/12/2010 21:30
UN Posto unico
Ingresso

call center   www.vivaticket.it   Punti vendita

24·1·11

Reflection about my Interview.
Yesterday I had my Interview at LCF. It wasn't that good. They were nice to me and it wasn't so hard I guess in a stressfull moment!!

There was Carole Cologni because they said it was and I gave the something   different and   and

I guess there were some papers sheets I didn't have enough! I just wish I could have more time to get everything READY... I think I arrived was too EARLY!!

Anyway it is done now I had my chance and I hope I used it at best!

→ ⊞ was one of the best evening & scary moments of my life!!!

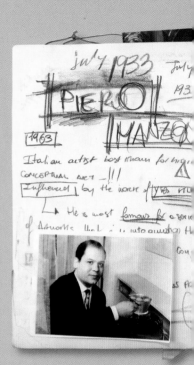

July 1933   July 193

PIERO   MANZO

1963

Italian artist best known for his CONCEPTUAL art —!!!
Influenced by the work of YVES KLE

→ He is most famous for a series of Artworks that into another He

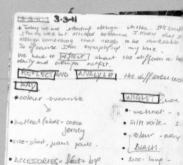

IMPASTATO DO A.
Westminster   → bug breakfast
→ buy bicycle
→ stay

WESTMINSTER →

I'M BACK

FINAL

3·3·11

• Today we are starting design clothes.

REFLECT AND ANALYSE

DAY
• colour -
• mustard fabric = cotton jersey
• size = short, jeans pants.
• ACCESSORIES = hats, bp bags —

NIGHT
• material =
• silk voile =
• colour - every BLACK
• size = long -
• ACCESSO

PREMIÈRE CLASSE
Accessory Designers Trade Show

OMM COLLECTION

EXPOSANT

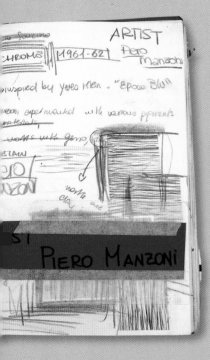

ARTIST

CHROME 1961-62 Piero Manzoni

inspired by Yves Klein. "Space Blu"

experimented with various pigments materials

works with gesso

PIERO MANZONI

USEUM "MAO"
TURIN

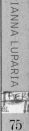

CAPSULE COLLECTION
20 dresses → day
→ night

ideas - jackets
ideas - trousers
ideas - shirts
ideas - tops
ideas - dresses

FIRST FASHION DRAW

TO DO
20 dresses
10 ideas jackets
10 ideas trousers
10 ideas 4 shirts
10 ideas 4 tops

PARIS FASHION WEEK

March 2011   REFLECTION ABOUT the WORK

→ This fear has been very important for couldes but not too much for selling. I think because they very very different from the rest of the stands.

joanna mandle

A MIX OF CHILD-LIKE INFLUENCES AND PLAYFUL CLOWNS COMBINE TO PRODUCE VISUALLY ENGAGING RESEARCH WHICH AIMS TO TELL A STORY OF CHILDHOOD INNOCENCE, JUXTAPOSED WITH A CONTEMPORARY SETTING. RESEARCH PROVIDES A SPRINGBOARD FOR IDEAS AND EXPERIMENTS WHICH JOANNA USES TO BRING HER DESIGNS UP-TO-DATE.

Crochet techniques taught
at christening museums

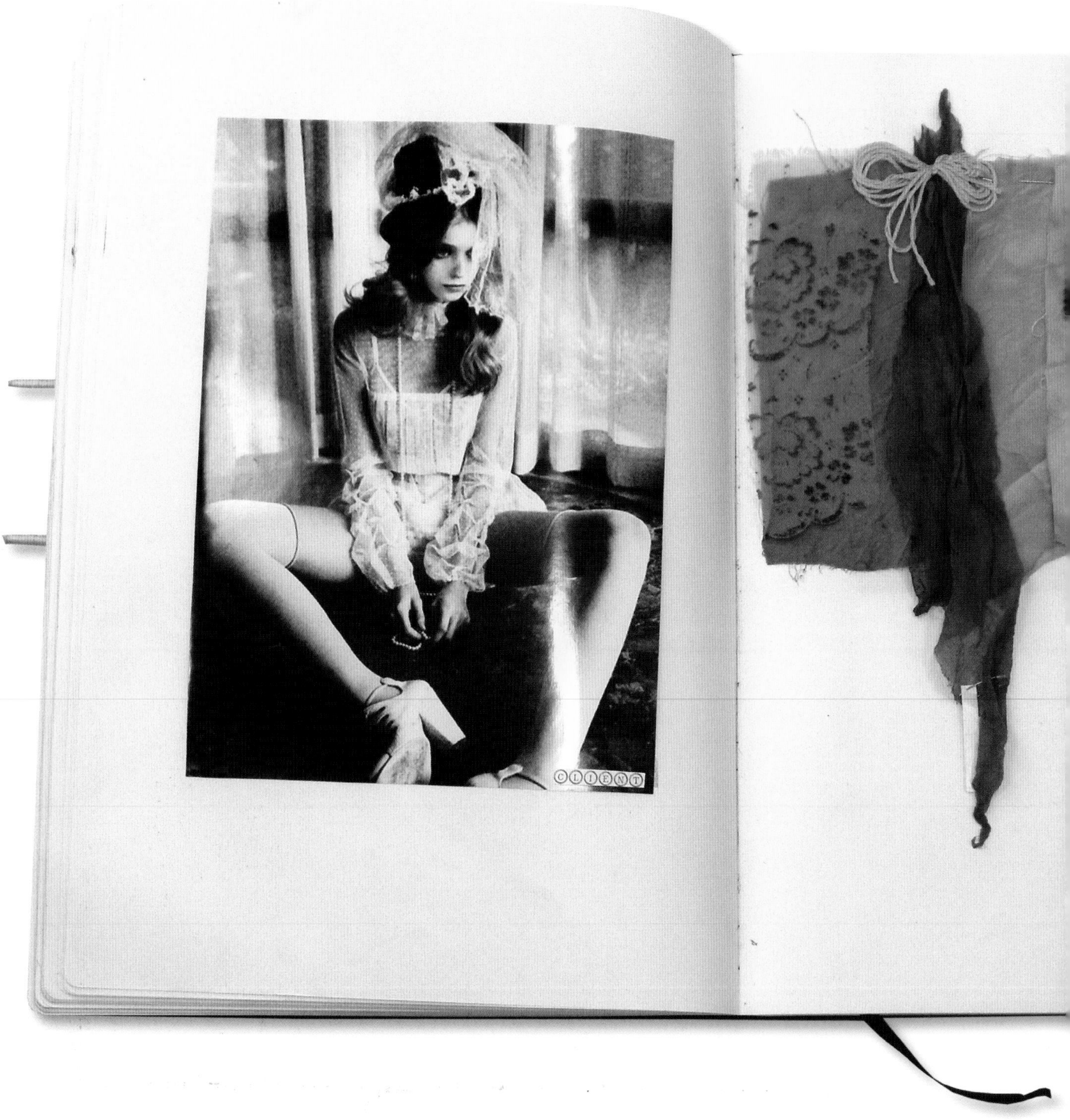
CLIENT

<< Working in this way allows me to extract details directly from the research to inform all aspects of my work, from pocket details to shape >>

elena occidente

THE FIRST PART OF ELENA'S RESEARCH PROCESS IS ABOUT COLLECTING LOTS OF VISUAL IMAGERY, THEN FINDING INTERESTING DETAILS WHICH SHE DEVELOPS INTO IDEAS. ELENA COMBINES RESEARCH WITH DRAWING AS HER INSPIRATION. SHE USES A MULTIMEDIA APPROACH WITHIN HER RESEARCH SKETCHBOOK TO PRODUCE FASCINATING AND ENGAGING PAGES.

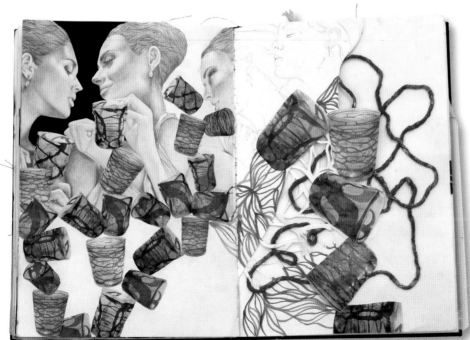

88

Insects

Look Inside

Look at the
HEAD

The mouthparts of the Fly are modified for SPONGING FOOD...

Sponging Insects...

compound eyes

Touch it...

<< *I like to visually tell a story in my research, which helps other people follow the journey in a fluent and interesting way* >>

A

Turn to mix the colors

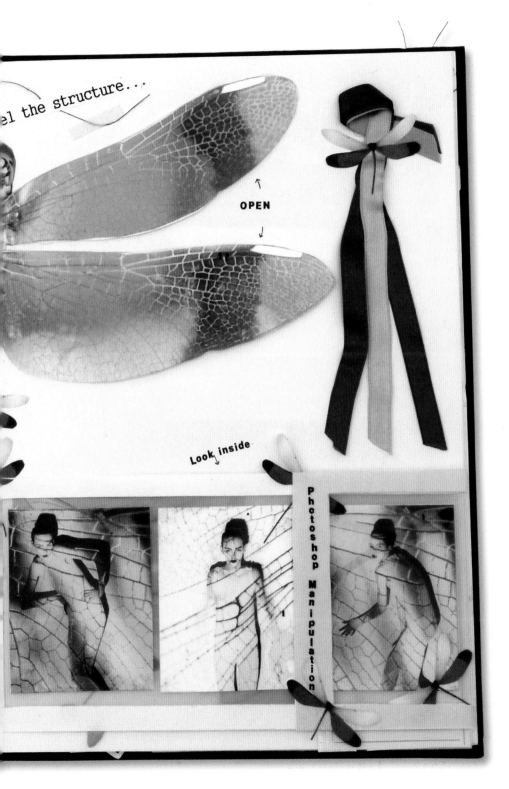

el the structure...

OPEN

Look inside

Photoshop Manipulation

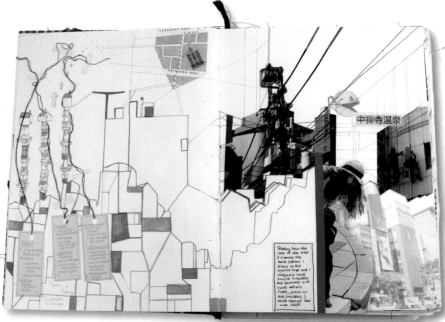

中禅寺温泉

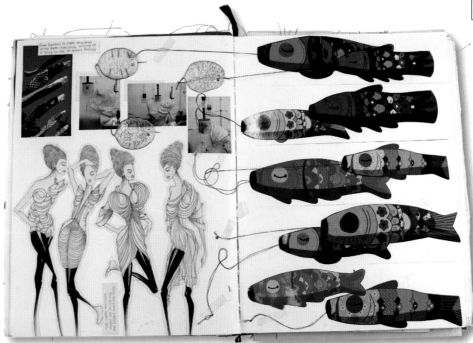

crimson o'shea

CRIMSON'S IDEAS ARE RAW AND FEARLESS, REFLECTING HER ABILITY TO CREATE CHALLENGING CLOTHING WHICH CONVEYS HER PERSONALITY. HER FIGURES ARE AWKWARD AND UNCOMFORTABLE, AND HER DESIGNS ARE LITERAL INTERPRETATIONS OF HER RESEARCH, WITH AN HISTORICAL ARCHITECTURAL DETAIL, FOR EXAMPLE, BECOMING AN IDEA FOR A SLEEVE.

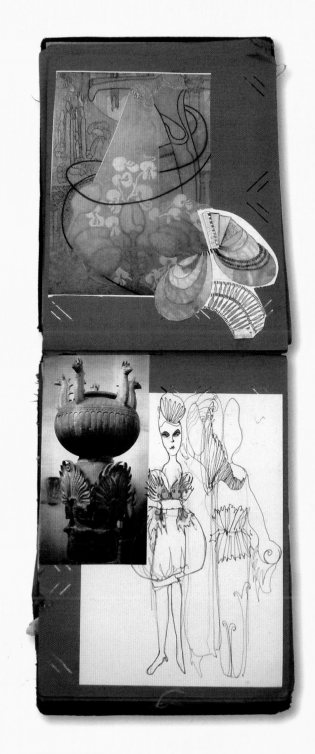

<< *I like seeing the world through my own eyes and interpreting what I see in my own way* >>

Greek Architecture

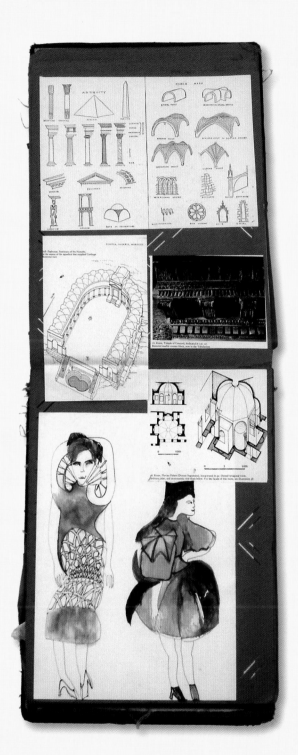

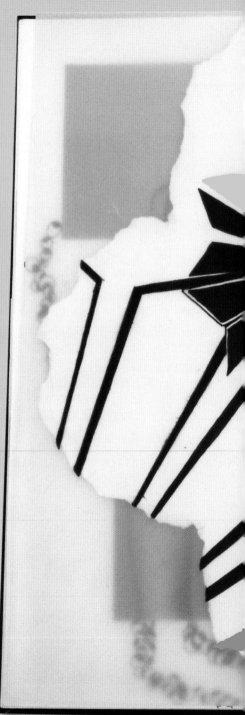

athos n romangoli ATHOS TAKES
INSPIRATION FROM UNCONVENTIONAL THEMES AND
OBJECTS TO CREATE STORIES AND CONCEPTS. HE USES
VISUAL IMAGERY TO HELP HIM DEVELOP AND EXPLORE
HIS IDEAS. HE ENJOYS MAKING HIS RESEARCH AN
ENGAGING VISUAL JOURNEY.

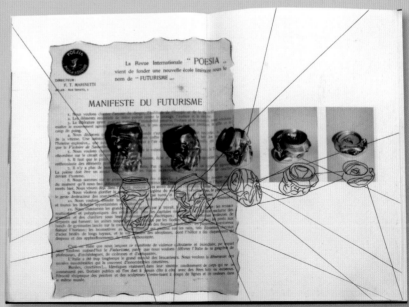

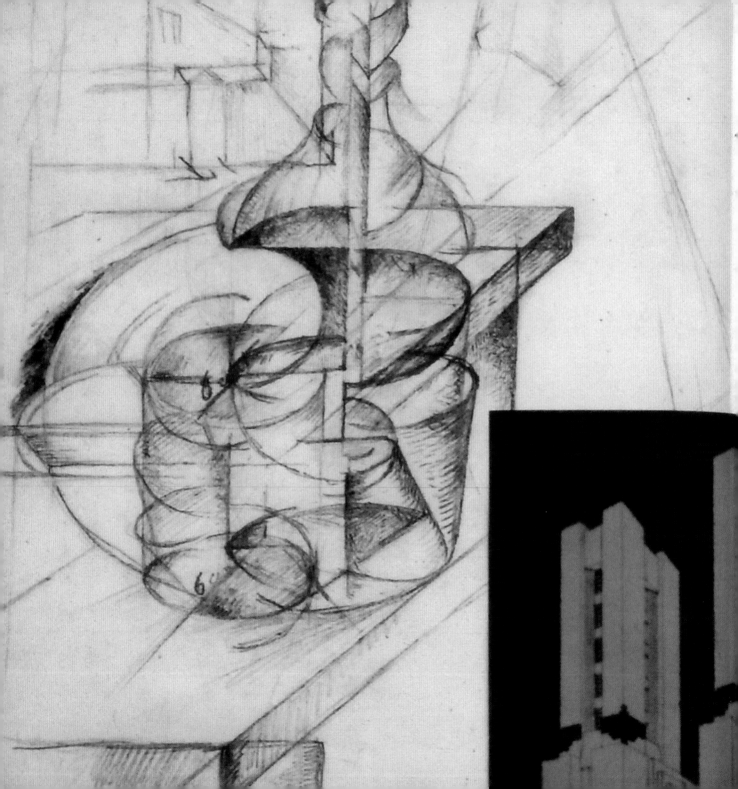

<< For me, research is perhaps the most important part of the process. When you create research, you can expand your ideas as much as you want >>

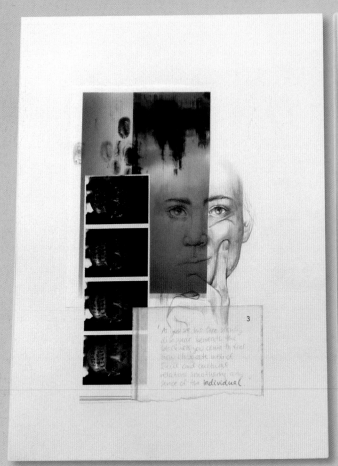

evelina romano
EVELINA LIKES TO EXPRESS MOODS AND EMOTIONS THROUGH HER ILLUSTRATIVE STYLE OF RESEARCH. SHE DELVES INTO HISTORICAL REFERENCES AND SEEKS SMALL DETAILS WHICH SHE THEN INTERPRETS INTO MAIN FEATURES ON GARMENTS. HER IDEAS ARE DEVELOPED IN A SLOW AND CONSIDERED MANNER.

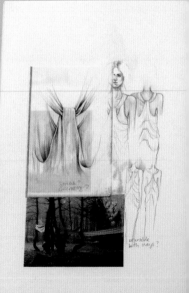

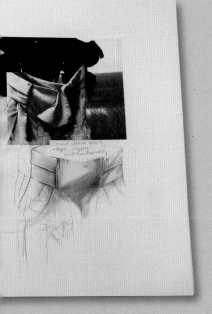

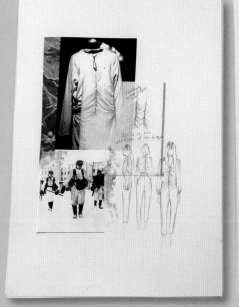

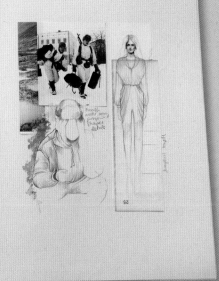

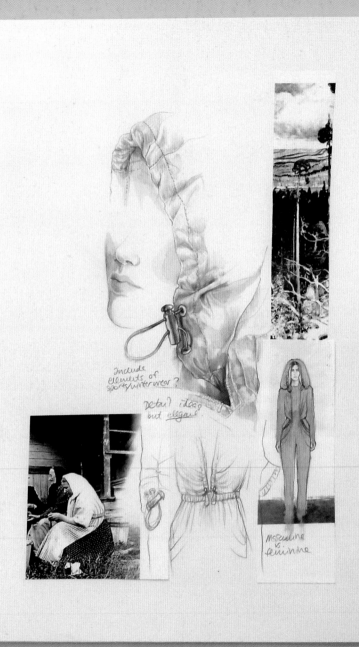

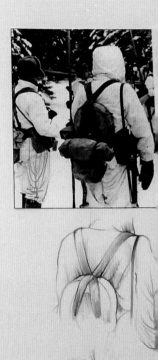

Include
elements of
sports/winterwear?

Detail ideas
but elegant.

Masculine
vs.
Feminine

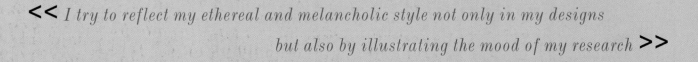

<< I try to reflect my ethereal and melancholic style not only in my designs
but also by illustrating the mood of my research >>

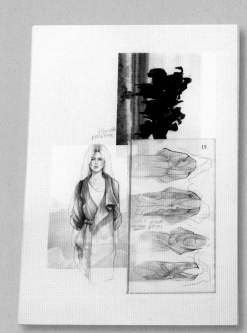

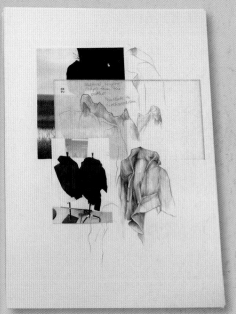

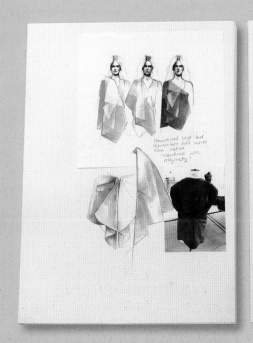

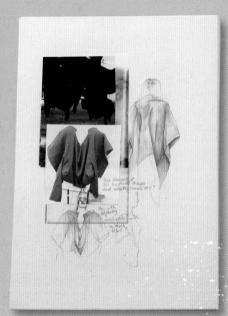

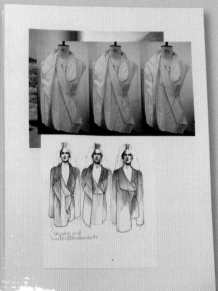

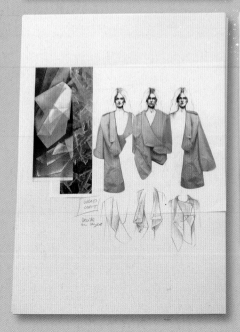

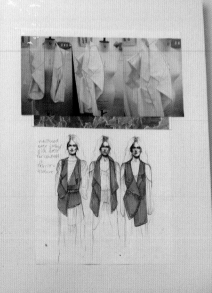

unconventional placement of
pockets, buttons, even sleeves?

Take elements of
the sculptural shapes
and create SYMMETRY?

Play with
asymmetry
cowl neck with
tailored
fabric?

kamran sarwar TRIBAL INFLUENCES MIXED WITH NATURAL MATERIALS ARE AMONGST SOME OF THE SOURCES KAMRAN LOOKS AT TO INSPIRE IDEAS FOR HIS WOMEN'S ACCESSORIES. HE USES HIS RESEARCH TO INSPIRE IDEAS ABOUT MATERIALS AND TRADITIONAL CRAFT TECHNIQUES WHICH HE INCORPORATES INTO HIS DESIGNS.

<< *The research process begins with finding an initial connection with a concept or thought, which I begin to understand and explore through the process of drawing and taking photographs* >>

Dende
Ear pendant
tortoise shell
pearl shell
dogs teeth
black banana
seed

PIG
HOG HAIR

dog teeth
or
shell
neck plates

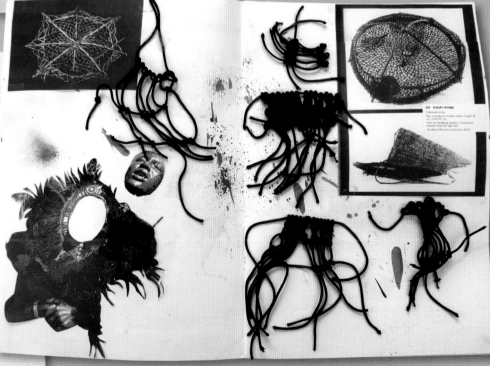

WARIDA
SORCERER of
FAMOUS FIGHT

leader of village militia
skin of red blanket attached
to nose, pig tails
boy hairs worn
hog horn

House of the Ancestors

NGHT OF
BiRDS

birds" and the earrings he wore at his circumcision. The women plait the cord for the initiates' headdresses, the initiates gut the birds, stuff the capes with grass and the men attach the birds to the cord by their bills. The then fix two ostrich feathers on either side of the headdress which the boys wear for the month following circumcision

A circumcised boy on the threshold of warriorhood, wearing the headdress of the "month o...

wearing capes of sheepskin blackened   with cow dung mixed with sheep fat.

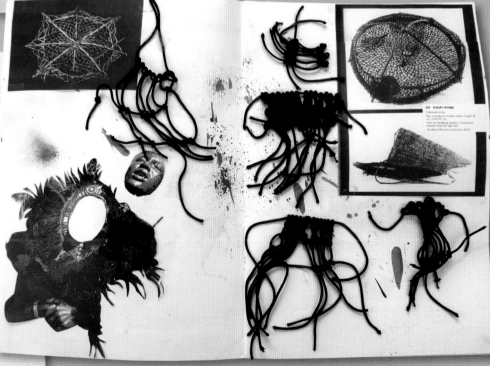

237 Kakuhi dredge

jessica sharpe JESSICA HAS AN EYE FOR DETAIL AND FINDS INSPIRATION IN THE
MINIMAL. SHE USES PHOTOGRAPHY TO MANIPULATE AND TEST IDEAS BEFORE TRYING LARGER
EXPERIMENTS ON THE MANNEQUIN STAND. JESSICA ENJOYS THE PROCESS OF EXPLORING
IDEAS AND PUSHING THE BOUNDARIES OF TEXTILE MANIPULATION AND THEN EXPANDING THIS
FURTHER THROUGH DESIGNING WOMENSWEAR.

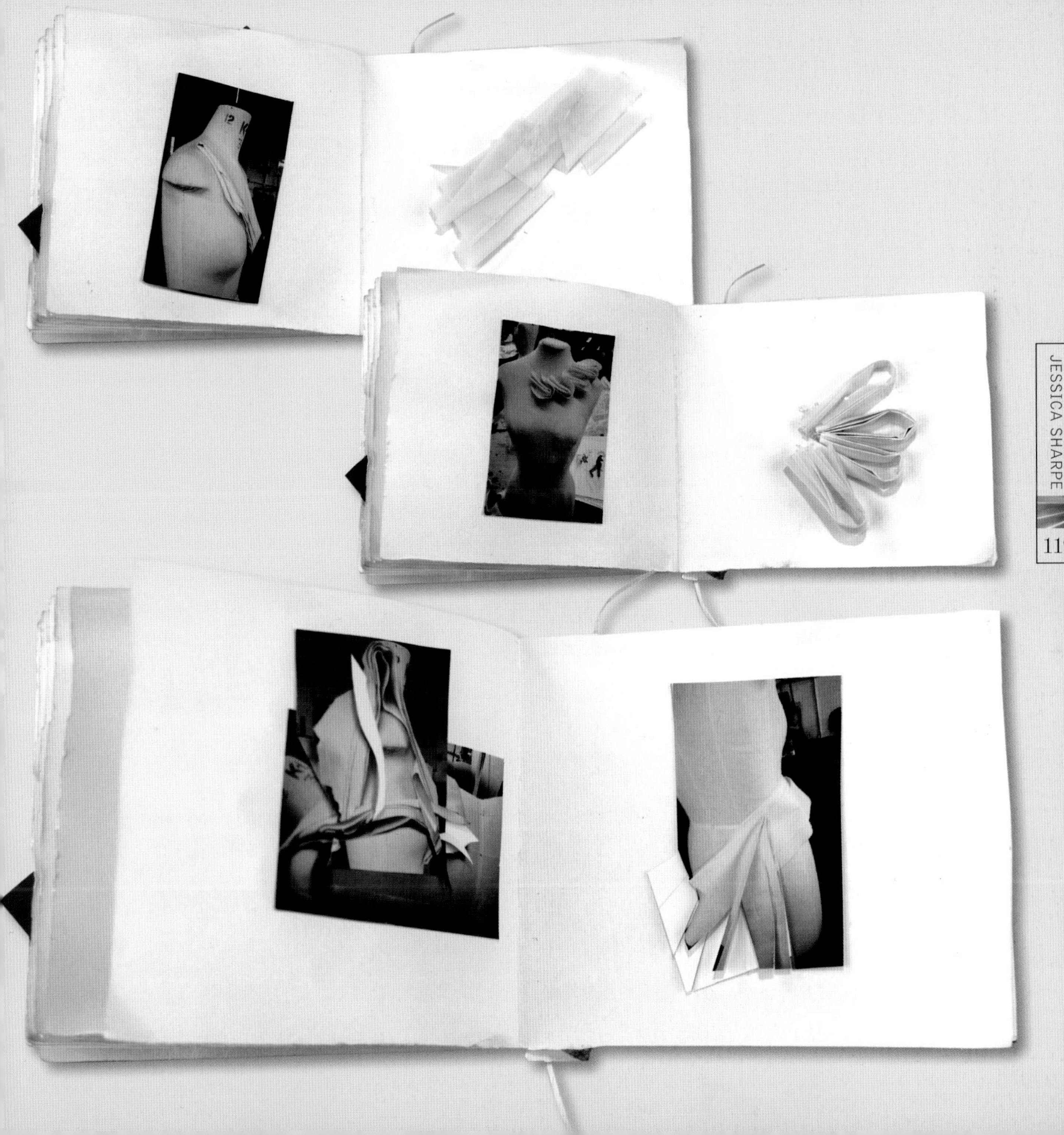

DESIGNING FROM MY PHOTOGRAPHS

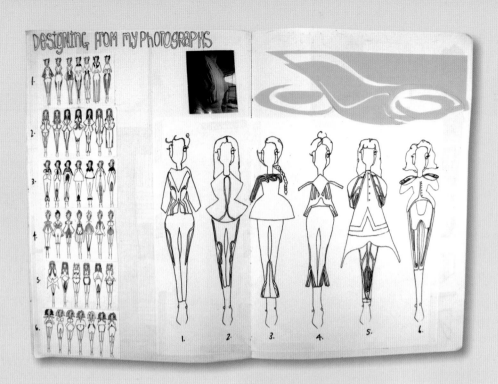

scale - making bigger and smaller...

recreate in fabric...

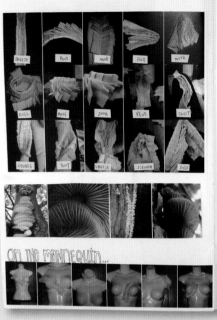

POSSibLE dEsigns...

ON THE MANNEQUIN...

diffERENT ANgLEs...

dEvELOPING USING PAPER...

RECREATING IN FABRIC...

<< *I work in a very individual way and use my own personal interpretations of different sources combined with a diverse range of media to generate ideas* >>

eddie siu
EDDIE LOOKS AT NATURALLY-OCCURRING LINES FOUND IN NATURE AND USES THIS AS HIS STARTING POINT TO APPROACH DESIGNING MENSWEAR. HE ALSO TAKES INSPIRATION FROM WESTERN TRIBES; IDEAS ABOUT STYLING. WEARABILITY AND PRACTICALITY ARE ESSENTIAL COMPONENTS IN THE DESIGN PROCESS.

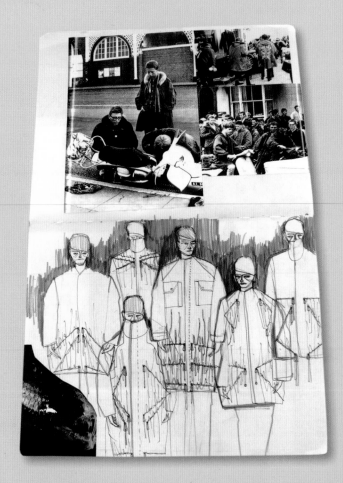

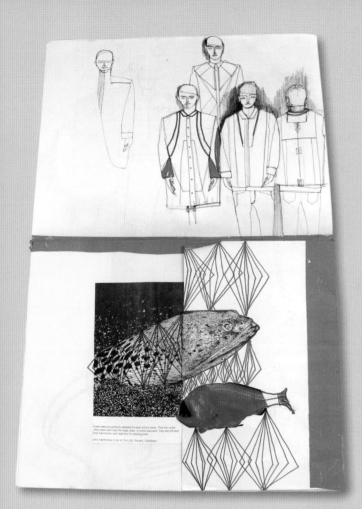

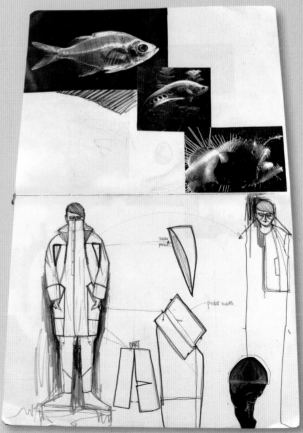

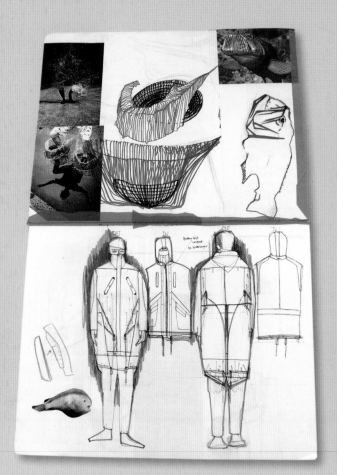

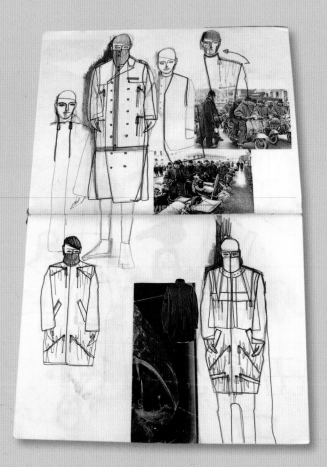

<< Simple forms found in nature are what inspire me, as well as seeing things in a new way >>

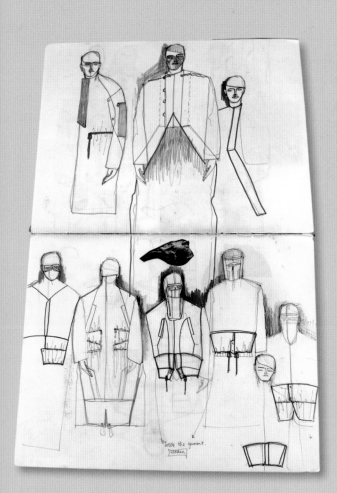

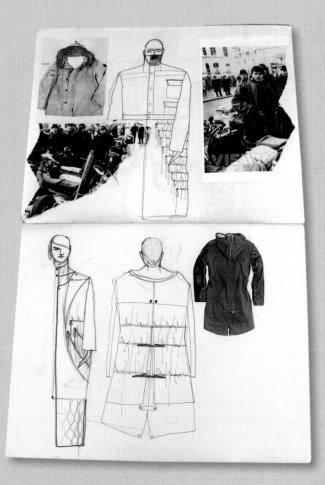

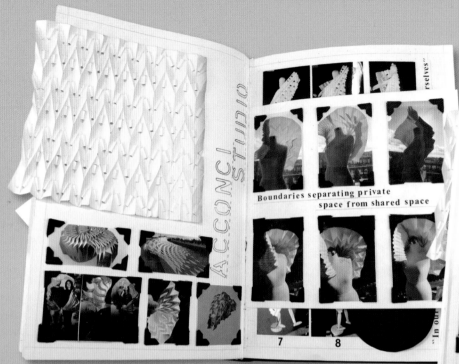

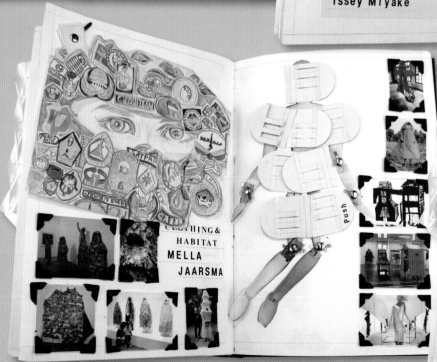

wen sun
MODERN ART, SCULPTURE AND LAYERING ARE THEMES PRESENT THROUGHOUT WEN'S WORK. SHE DEVELOPS HER RESEARCH BY EXPERIMENTING ON THE MANNEQUIN STAND. WEN LIKES TO DESIGN IN A WAY THAT MAKES THE WEARER FEEL LIKE A PART OF THE INITIAL INSPIRATION.

3 2 1

4 5 6

7 8 9

7 8 9

ARE
WE
TRAPP

Anti Form

Morris

Robert

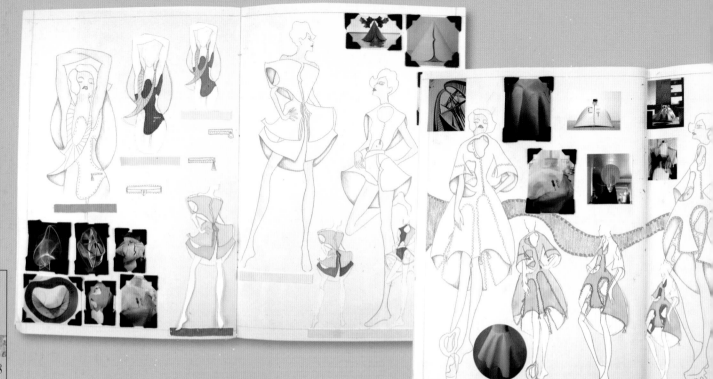

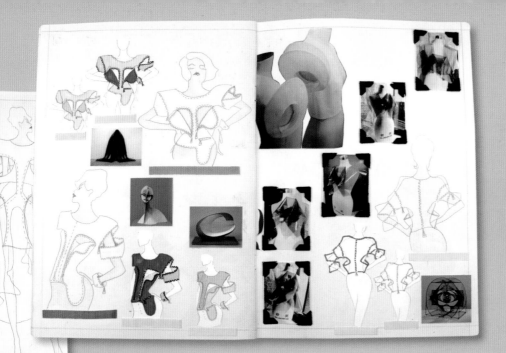

<< *I have a habit of collecting pictures of everything that inspires me no matter whether they link to my research topic or not* >>

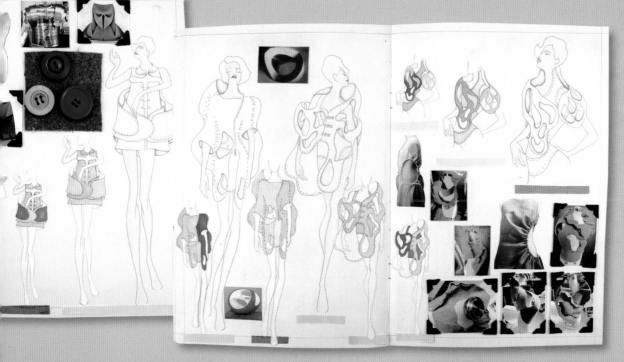

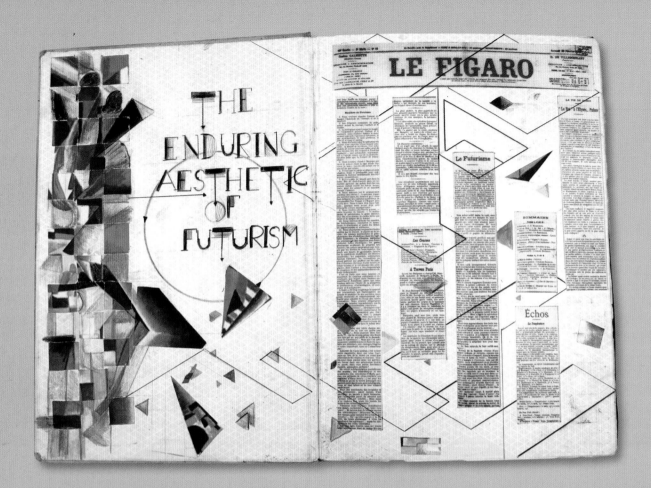

daniel tanner
DANIEL LIKES THE CHALLENGE OF STRONG THEMES TO INTERPRET INTO IDEAS FOR FASHION DESIGN. HE INCLUDES LOTS OF CONTEXTUAL AND POLITICAL REFERENCES TO EXPAND HIS RESEARCH AND HELP HIM DEVELOP HIS THOUGHTS AND IDEAS. HIS METHODS OF WORKING IN RESEARCH SKETCHBOOKS ARE SYMPATHETIC TO THE SUBJECT; HE THEN EXTRACTS THE VISUAL CONTENT TO USE AS A SPRINGBOARD FOR HIS DESIGNS.

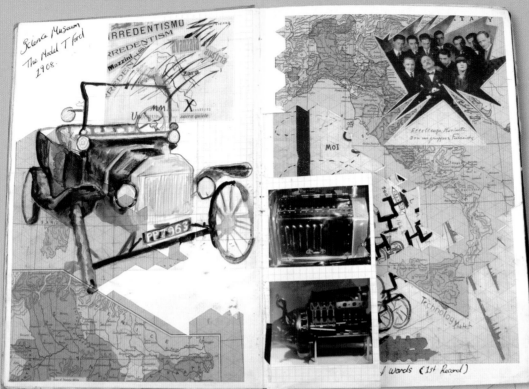

Science Museum
The Model T Ford
1908.

IRREDENTISMO
IRREDENTISM
Mazzini
avanzata austria
Zara

MOI

Eccellenza Marinetti
a un gruppo di Futuristi

Technology

...f words (1st Record)

F. T. MARINETTI FUTURISTA
ZANG
TUMB TUMB
ADRIANOPOLI OTTOBRE 1912
TUUUMB IN LIBERTA
PAROLE Tümb Tümb Tümb

META ANALYSIS.

Of Umberto Boccioni's Unique Forms of Continuity in Space. Inspiration: Irregular forms interacting, interfering with the figure.

Additive Colour theory of light

DRAWINGS.

1. ETCHELLS.
2. ATKINSON
3. BOMBERG.
4. WADSWORTH.

supriya thukral SUPRIYA'S RESEARCH
DEVELOPS BEYOND THE ORIGINAL IDEA AND
ENCOMPASSES A VARIETY OF CONTEXTUAL LINKS
WHICH HELP HER TO BROADEN AND EXPAND
HER THOUGHTS. SHE ENJOYS THE PROCESS OF
TRANSLATING HER RESEARCH INTO IDEAS AND
GARMENTS FOR THE FEMALE BODY.

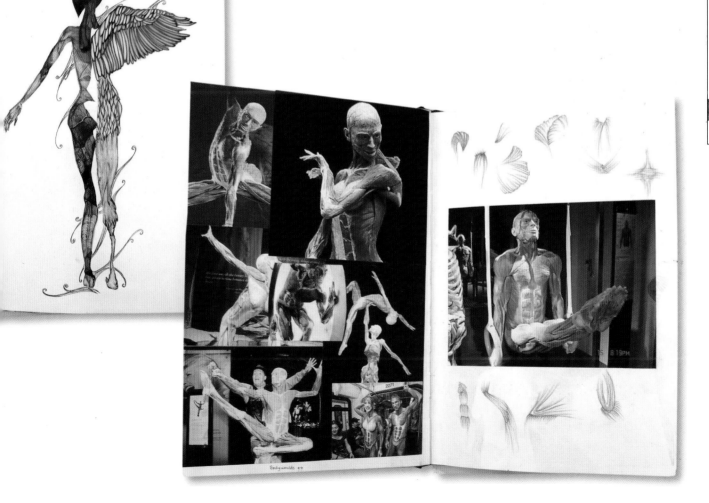

<< Researching an idea gives me the opportunity to look at art, architecture, literature, music and science >>

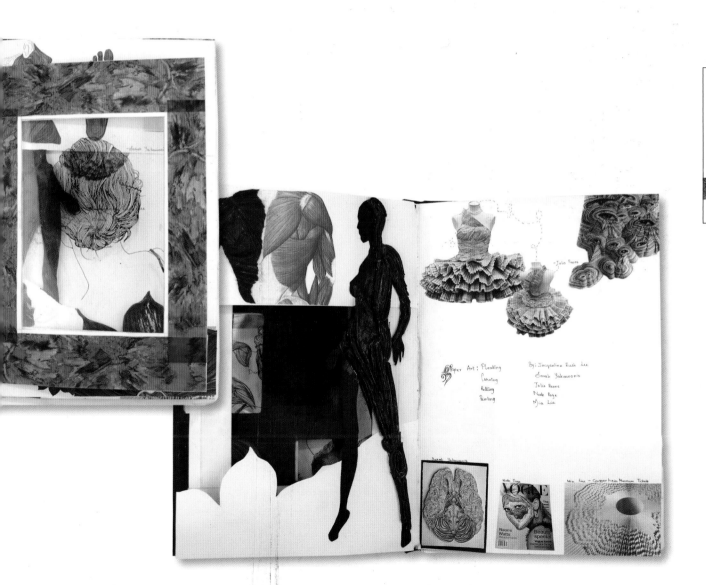

susanna wen

SUSANNA USES RESEARCH TO CHART HER DISCOVERIES. SHE ENJOYS EXPLORING ALL ASPECTS OF HER RESEARCH AREA AND LIKES TO CHALLENGE HERSELF BY DELVING INTO THE UNEXPECTED. SHE TAKES A MULTIMEDIA APPROACH TO PRODUCE PAGES WHICH CONVEY HER IDEAS, THOUGHTS AND JOURNEY.

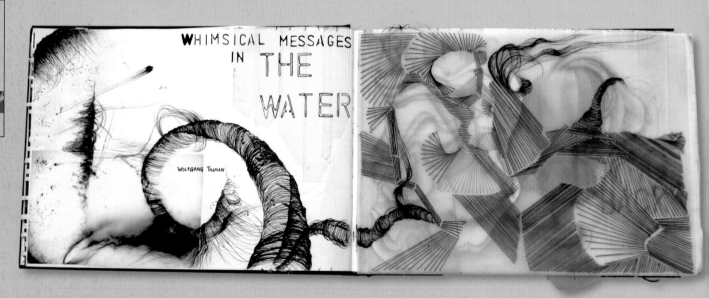

<< *I find the more obscure or unexpected the inspiration, the more original ideas that spring from it* >>

I TRY 2 GET IN 2 THE RHYTHM I start trying to make some pathetic little human marks that might have something to do with the MYSTERY of the GREAT, GREAT thing in front of us......

Sound Wave
Jean Shin

Experiments on the
mannequin

BLOG

PRINCE PELAYO

KILT!

KATE LOVES

MEXICAN
PATTERN

CHAVI

LAYERED
DENIM.

FLORAL
ON
A MAN!!

→ CARRIE
FROM
SEX + THE CITY

CIRCLES

WORKSHOP

CREATING
FABULOUS
SHAPES WITH
CIRCLES

tracey wong
HER WORK IS LARGELY INSPIRED BY A MUSE THAT LIVES IN HER MIND. SHE GIVES CHARACTER TO HER MUSE AND WATCHES AS SHE BECOMES MORE THAN JUST A FIGMENT OF HER IMAGINATION. TRACEY IS ALSO INTERESTED IN CUTTING AND GARMENT DETAILS AND THE EXPERIENCES OF THE WEARER.

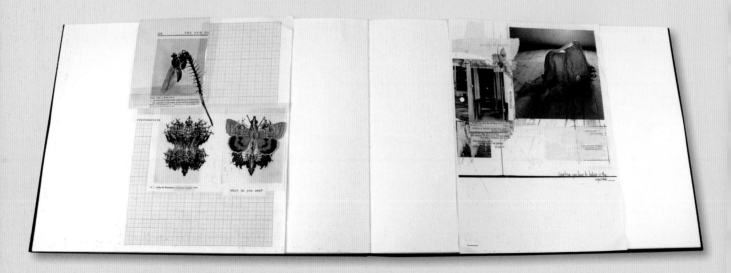

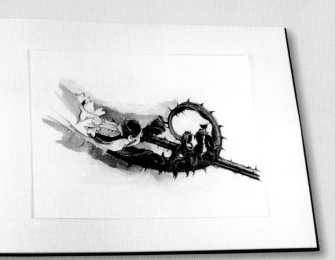

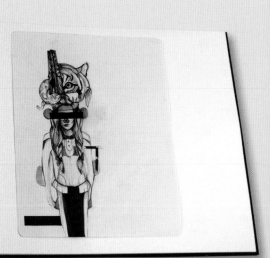

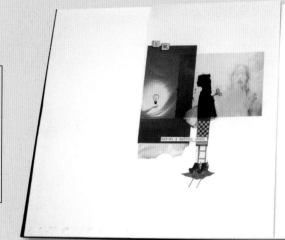

<< *I work with juxtaposing found images and drawing to create something that is personal and invites the viewer to develop their own conclusions* >>

qian wu

QIAN EXPLORES HER RESEARCH TOPIC THROUGH ALL POSSIBLE AVENUES. SHE MIXES BOLD COLOURS WITH UNCONVENTIONAL APPROACHES TO DESIGN FOR INTERESTING AND UNUSUAL RESULTS. SHE FINDS THE FREEDOM OF RESEARCH ALLOWS HER THE SPACE TO EXPLORE BEFORE DISTILLING HER DESIGNS.

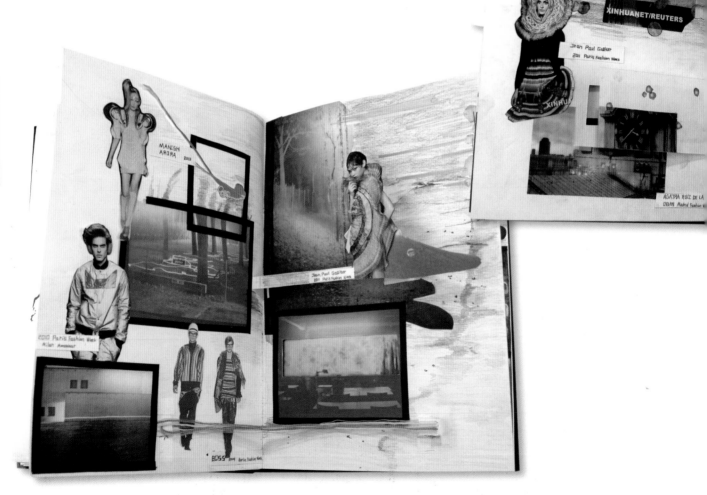

<< *Challenging themes move me into action. I love the process of finding what's out there* >>

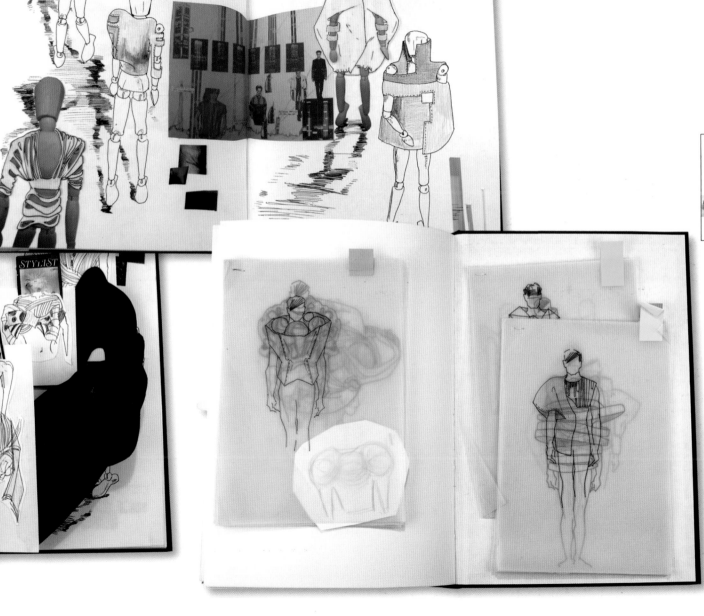

guidong yang JUXTAPOSITING IMAGES AND IDEAS AND REINTERPRETING THE
MUNDANE INTO SOMETHING INTERESTING, GUIDONG USES EVERYDAY OBJECTS, OVERLAYS
AND PLAYS WITH DRAWING. HE USES BOLD COLOURS THROUGHOUT TO ACHIEVE HIS LOOK,
DEVELOPING IDEAS THROUGH LAYERING AND DRAWING.

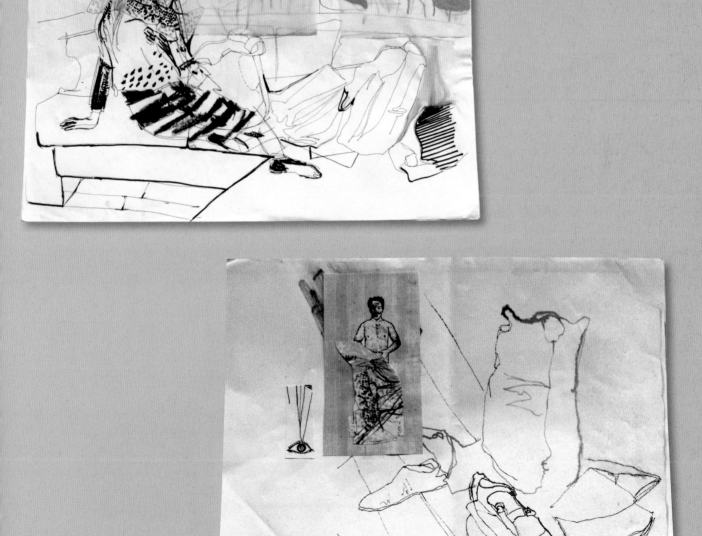

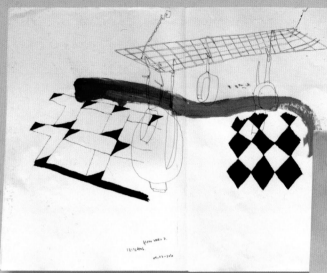

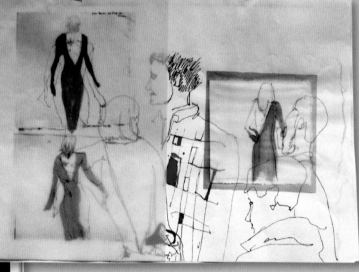

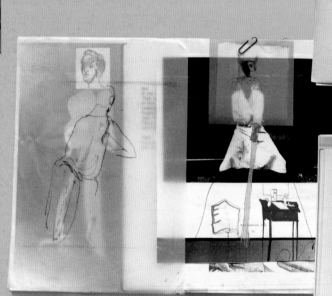

Saturday night at the Bijou.

Harry tried his first love, the theater, but the current cultural thing was Heat and Light. Purged of actors and stages everyone did his own thing in this Canned Theater.

'You'd get the same sensations if you moved a dry cleaning plant into a Sauna,' . . sneered Harry.

<< *I take my everyday life as inspiration,*
using drawing to capture and
collect interesting elements of
what I see >>

conclusion

CREATIVITY AND IDEAS EMERGE from original thought. Within the confines of a research sketchbook thought can expand without any restrictions.

Without creativity, we would be devoid of original ideas and simply regurgitate what already existed.

Throughout the journey of working on this book, the one thing that continued to surpirse and delight me was the individuality that emerged for each person's research sketchbook. The individual personalities and creative voice is what is captured within the pages of research sketchbooks.

In the age of the internet, blogs, websites and social networking, the creativity and quality found within research sketchbooks can never be replicated online. My hope for the future is that students continue to research using sketchbooks. I hope they continue to draw and paint and sew and use their hands to create and manipulate, to discover, question, re-question and develop new ideas.

Whether you are a novice or a professional, it's good to be reminded of the very things that got us all so excited about fashion in the first place. Individuality in research comes from personal response and finding your own voice. Its may take a few research sketchbooks before you discover it but in the meantime, enjoy the journey, it's fun.

blogs/websites

www.japanesestreets.com
Japanese street fashion pictures

ww.refinery29.com/everywhere
Fashion/shopping/lifestyle based in New York

www.elle.com
Fashion magazine website

www.magmabooks.com
London based book shop

www.jeanettesshop.blogspot.com
Emerging fashion designers in London

www.doverstreetmarket.com
Designer label mens and womens clothes and
accessories inLondon

www.darkroomlondon.com
Exclusive fashion accessories and interiors in
London

www.beyondthevalley.com
Clothes shop for emerging designers in West
End London

www.bstorelondon.com
Clothes/lifestyle store in London

www.anniesvintageclothing.co.uk
In Camden, London

www.alfiesantiques.com
Antiques market in London

www.dazeddigital.com
Fashion/arts website

www.vogue.co.uk
Fashion website

www.thecoolhunter.net
General fashion and life style bible

showstudio.com
Fashion/arts website/blog

fashionista.com
Fashion website

www.treehugger.com
Sustainable art/fashion/lifestyle

www.myfashionlife.com
Fashion website/news/fashion updates

www.style.com
Catwalk news/updates/shows

www.takashimaya.co.jp
Fashion department store in Japan, stocking
designer labels from around the world.

www.designersnexus.com
Online resource for aspiring fashion designers

www.mifashionblog.com
Fashion blog

www.lookatme.ru
Russian website

www.businessoffashion.com
Canadian business mans fashion blog/site

thesartorialist.blogspot.com
Fashion blog-pictures of people on the street

stylebubble.typepad.com
British blogger

www.myfashionlife.com
British website/blog

www.threadbanger.com
DIY fashion website

theimagist.com
Styling website

thefashionisto.com
Men's modelling site

www.omiru.com
Fashion website

www.sassybella.com
Fashion website

www.fashionsquad.com
Fashion blog

fashioncopious.typepad.com
Fashion blog

kingdomofstyle.typepad.co.uk/my_weblog
Fashion blog

www.geometricsleep.com
Fashion blog

www.theclotheswhisperer.co.uk
Fashion blog

www.fashiontrendsetter.com
Fashion trends website

www.peclersparis.com
Fashion trend website

further reading

Faerm, Steven. *Fashion Design Course: Principles, Practice and Techniques: The Ultimate Guide for Aspiring Fashion Designers*. Thames & Hudson, 2010.

Greenlees, Kay. *Creating Sketchbooks for Embroiderers and Textile Artists: Exploring the Embroiderers' Sketchbook*. Batsford Ltd., 2005.

Gaimster, Julia. *Visual Research Methods in Fashion*. Berg Publishers, 2011.

Perrella, Lynne. *Artists' Journal and Sketchbooks: Exploring and Creating Personal Pages*. Rockport Publishers, 2007.

O'Donnell, Timothy. *Sketchbook: Conceptual Drawings From The Worlds Most Influential Designers and Creatives*. Rockport Publishers, 2009.

Grandon, Adrian and Fitzgerald, Tracey. *200 Projects to Get You into Fashion Design*. A&C Black Publishers, 2009.

Rothman, Julia. *Drawn In: A Peek into the Inspiring Sketchbooks of 45 Fine Artists, Illustrators, Graphic Designers, and Cartoonists*. Quarry Books, 2011.

Seivewright, Simon. *Basics Fashion Design: Research and Design*. AVA Publishing, 2007.

Udale, Jenny. *Basics Fashion Design 02: Textiles and Fashion*. AVA Publishing, 2008.

Chakrabarti, Nina. *My Wonderful World of Fashion: A Book for Drawing, Creating and Dreaming*. Laurence King, 2009.

Duburg, Annette and van der Tol, Rixt. *Draping: art and craftsmanship in fashion design*. De Jong Honde, 2008.

Vinken, Barbara and Hewson, Mark. *Fashion Zeitgeist: Trends and Cycles in the Fashion System*. Berg Publishers, 2004.

Burke, Sandra. *Fashion Entrepreneur: Starting Your Own Fashion Business*. Burke Publishing, 2008.

Ireland, Patrick John. *Fashion Design Drawing and Presentation*. Batsford Ltd., 1982.

Nunnelly, Carol A. *Fashion Illustration School: A Complete Handbook for Aspiring Designers and Illustrators*. Thames & Hudson, 2009.

Morris, Bethan. *Fashion Illustrator (Portfolio)*. Laurence King, 2010.

Wesen Bryant, Michelle. *Fashion Drawing: Illustration Techniques for Fashion Designers*. Laurence King 2011.

Schuman, Scott. *The Sartorialist*. Penguin, 2009.